Talking Politics?

What You Need to Know *before* Opening Your Mouth

Other Titles of Interest

Talking Politics?

What You Need to Know *before* Opening Your Mouth

Sheila Suess Kennedy

GEORGETOWN UNIVERSITY PRESS

Library of Congress Cataloging-in-Publication Data

Names: Kennedy, Sheila Suess, author.
Title: Talking politics? : what you need to know before opening your mouth / Sheila Suess Kennedy.
Description: Washington, DC : Georgetown University Press, 2016.
Identifiers: LCCN 2016007107 (print) | LCCN 2016008599 (ebook) | ISBN 9781626163782 (pb : alk. paper) | ISBN 9781626161450 (eb) | ISBN 9781626161450 ()
Subjects: LCSH: United States—Politics and government.
Classification: LCC JK31 .K45 2016 (print) | LCC JK31 (ebook) | DDC 320.973—dc23
LC record available at http://lccn.loc.gov/2016007107

17 16   9 8 7 6 5 4 3 2 First printing

Printed in the United States of America

This publication was originally released as born-digital content. The links attached to the bolded words in the digital edition are not available in this print edition. Please refer to the ebook to access the linking features.

Contents

Introduction

As Daniel Patrick Moynihan famously observed, we are all entitled to our own opinions but not to our own facts. Arguments based on manufactured histories or distorted realities are intellectually dishonest and ultimately unproductive—and they are particularly destructive in an era when there is no universally trusted "mainstream" media to correct spin, misrepresentations, and outright lies.

This brief publication identifies some of the most common areas of confusion or misunderstanding—those distortions of accepted history, economics, and science that seem most often to characterize our contemporary political/social arguments—and distinguishes between *facts* that have been documented and agreed to by responsible people of all ideological perspectives and the different *conclusions* and *interpretations* that may be drawn from those facts. To use an analogy from the courtroom, two sides to a conflict may "stipulate" to what happened but then proceed to argue in good faith about what those agreed-to stipulations really tell us.

Why do we say that agreement on definitions and documented facts is important? Take the recent debates about the Affordable Care Act—aka "Obamacare"—as an example. People may have very different opinions about the wisdom of the policy choices involved, but a decision to repeal, implement, or amend the act depends upon agreement about what it actually says and does. If opposition to the policy is based upon "death panels" that don't exist, or if its defense is based upon an insistence that the individual

1

mandate isn't government coercion, the likelihood of reasoned discussion—let alone agreement on policy changes—disappears.

Or take the ongoing battles over religion in the nation's schools. There are genuine arguments to be made about the proper application of the Establishment Clause in the context of public education. But just as we can't have those reasoned disputes with people who insist that the First Amendment doesn't require separation of church and state, we cannot have productive conversations with people who insist that all the Founders were Deists who believed religion was unimportant.

Basing one's arguments on verifiable fact and accepted history actually helps people make more persuasive cases for their own points of view. We all encounter people who have a legitimate point worth considering, but who—because they are basing their argument on erroneous facts, or demonstrating a lack of understanding of important basic concepts—get dismissed out of hand. Credibility requires verifiable evidence. You might want to use that perfect quote from Thomas Jefferson that you saw on the internet, but if it is bogus, you've just undermined your own position. Defending alternate realities is like arguing about whether a fork is a spoon—it doesn't get you any closer to a useful resolution.

This brief work contains basic facts about the US Constitution, economic concepts and systems, and the nature of science and the scientific method that every citizen should know—facts and definitions that can serve as solid starting points from which you can build more persuasive arguments for your preferred policies, whatever they may be.

CHAPTER 1

What Everyone Should Know about the Constitution and American Legal System

What Is Government?

THIS MAY SEEM like a silly question, but in an age of outsourcing and privatization, it's often harder to identify "government" than you might think. For example, tax dollars pay the salaries of more than 18 million people employed by private companies or nonprofit organizations under contracts with government agencies. Are they part of the government? It depends.

Governments were originally defined as entities having the exclusive right to exercise *legitimate* coercive power. They were established to keep the peace and control the kinds of behaviors that a given society believes to be inconsistent with public order. It is a truism that a government strong enough to protect us is a government strong enough to oppress us, and some of our most acrimonious debates arise from concerns that by giving the government enough authority to do particular jobs, we may be giving it the power to unduly limit our liberties.

The government—sometimes referred to as "the state" (not to be confused with states like Indiana or California) or the "public sector" (not to be confused with "the public square," a very different concept)—is also a mechanism through which we citizens collectively do things that would be difficult or impossible to do individually, such as issue currency, defend the nation's borders, clean up waterways, or pave roads. There are two nongovernmental sectors: nonprofit and voluntary organizations or associations (sometimes called civil society or the nonprofit sector), and private persons, families, and businesses (the private sector).

The role of the government has grown significantly over the years, and thanks to new agencies performing new tasks and the growth of public–private partnerships of various kinds, its presence isn't always obvious. But here's a good rule of thumb: If an agency is managed by someone we've elected, or by someone appointed by someone we've elected, and if it is financed with our tax dollars, it's probably part of the government.

Why It Matters

In the United States, it is particularly important that we know the government when we see it because our constitutional system is largely based on a concept of "negative liberty." The Founders believed that **individual rights do not come from the government; rather, they are "natural."** We are entitled to certain rights simply by virtue of being human (thus the term "human rights"), and the government must respect and protect those rights. The US Bill of Rights is essentially a list of things that the government—"the state"—is forbidden to do. For example, the state cannot prescribe our religious or political beliefs, search us without probable cause, or censor our expression—and it is forbidden from doing these things *even when* popular majorities favor such actions.

Those limitations don't apply to private, nongovernmental actors. The government can't control what you read, for example, but while you were growing up, your mother could. The government can't tell you what to say but (at least at work) your boss can. Your public (government) school can't make you say a prayer, but a private or parochial school can. The doctrine known as "state action" is shorthand for these limits on government intrusions. If the government hasn't acted, or isn't involved, neither is the Constitution. Private actors can break other laws, like civil rights laws, but *only the government can violate the Bill of Rights.* That makes it pretty important to be able to recognize when the government has acted.

What Is a Constitution?

Constitutions are different *in kind* from the statutes and ordinances passed by legislative bodies. They are statements of broad principles that govern and limit what kind of laws legislatures may properly enact and what sort of actions government officials can properly take. While parts of the US Constitution deal with specific practical matters—how old must someone be to run for president? What is the function of the courts?—such matters also are statements of important principles meant to guide and constrain lawmakers and government authorities in the future. There is a very big difference between "There shall be a traffic signal at First and Main Streets" or "There will be no smoking in public places" and "The right of the people to be secure in their persons, houses, papers, and effects, against unreason-able searches and seizures, shall not be violated." A government is said to be *legitimate* when its laws and the actions of its public officials are consistent with the principles of its constitution.

The US Constitution was our second try at a national charter. The 1781 **Articles of Confederation** were the product of states jealous of their sovereignty and unwilling to give the central government authority to do many things a national government needed to do. Under the Articles, the US government had only those powers the states relinquished, and it lacked the power to enforce decisions with which states disagreed. It even lacked taxing power; it could ask the states to "contribute," but it couldn't compel payment. The Constitution that replaced the Articles created a much more robust central government.

Two hundred plus years after the current American Constitution was drafted, lawmakers and judges must consult the text and context of our Constitution in order to decide what the drafters' original intentions were and the nature of the values they were trying to protect. Since there were many participants in the Constitutional Congress, and they did not speak with one voice, there were often differences of opinion about the meaning of the various provisions of the Constitution and Bill of Rights even then.

Why It Matters

Understanding the difference between a constitution and an ordinary law is important for a number of reasons, not the least of which is that constitu-tions are statements of national aspirations and beliefs about the proper way for citizens to live together. Understanding what values the Founders were trying to protect helps us apply those values to situations they could never have envisioned. It's a safe bet that James Madison did not have an opinion about government regulation of pornography on the internet, for example. But he most certainly had strong opinions about the value of protecting free expression. The Founders who drafted the **Fourth Amend-ment's search and seizure provisions** could hardly have foreseen technol-ogy that allows police officers to "see" marijuana growing inside a house from across the street. Our courts must decide how the Founders would have applied the *principles* that were so important to them to such new "facts on the ground." This process is what legal scholars mean when they talk about the "living Constitution." If we don't know the history and philosophy that motivated the Founders' choices, we can't form educated opinions about the application of their principles to modern situations.

What Was the Enlightenment?

The Enlightenment is the name given to the eighteenth-century cultural, intellectual, and philosophical movement that produced science, empirical inquiry, and the "natural rights" and "social contract" theories of government legitimacy on which our system is based. Enlightenment thinkers include Isaac Newton, Voltaire, Montesquieu, Thomas Hobbes, Adam Smith, John Stuart Mill, John Locke, and many others. The Enlightenment ushered in profound changes in the way people thought about science, education, liberty, and the role of the government.

Why It Matters

The Enlightenment changed the definition of liberty. The Puritans and Pilgrims who came to America defined religious liberty as "freedom to do the right thing"—freedom to worship and obey the *right* God in the *true* church, and to use the power of the government to ensure that their neighbors did too. The Founders who crafted our Constitution some 150 years later were products of the Enlightenment and its dramatically different concept of liberty. Enlightenment philosophers defined liberty as *personal autonomy*—an individual's freedom to make his own moral and political decisions, free of government coercion. In the Enlightenment's libertarian construction, liberty meant freedom to "do your own thing" so long as you did not thereby harm the person or property of someone else, and so long as you recognized the equal right of others to do *their* "own thing." The US Constitution is based upon the Enlightenment understanding of liberty.

The Enlightenment also gave us **John Locke's** "social contract" theory of government. Locke believed that government legitimacy rested on a theorized agreement—a "social contract"—between citizens and their governments. Citizens gave the state a monopoly on the use of coercive power in return for the state's protection of their property, and the state's maintenance of public order and safety. This was a dramatic change from belief in the divine right of kings, a belief that had long justified monarchy. In Locke's view—adopted by the Founders—power came from the people, who authorized the government to exercise that power for specific purposes, and who could *revoke* that authority if the government failed to keep its part of the bargain.

What Is the Bill of Rights?

When the Constitutional Convention drafted a document to replace the unworkable Articles of Confederation, that document did not include a Bill of Rights. The omission was not because there was a disagreement over the importance of those rights; it was because the new government was seen as an authority exercising only such powers as had been *delegated* to it, and those powers did not include censoring speech, dictating religious beliefs, and otherwise infringing fundamental liberties. Those who opposed adding written guarantees to the Constitution also worried that any effort to enumerate or list basic liberties would inevitably omit some. Nevertheless, it quickly became clear that the new Constitution would not be ratified unless proponents promised to enact a **Bill of Rights** spelling out specific liberties that the government could not infringe.

As passed, the first eight Amendments listed rights that the government was specifically forbidden to infringe; the **Ninth** and **Tenth** Amendments were added to address the concerns of Founders like Alexander Hamilton, who worried that any list of protected rights would inevitably leave some out. The Ninth and Tenth Amendments—sometimes called the Rights and Powers Amendments—were intended to make it clear that just because a right wasn't enumerated did not mean people didn't still have that right, and to affirm that powers not specifically given to the federal government were retained by the states or by the people.

The Bill of Rights initially limited only *federal* government action. It wasn't until the Fourteenth Amendment was ratified, in the wake of the Civil War, that the Bill of Rights' limits on government power were applied to state and local government actors as well. The **Fourteenth Amendment** prohibited states from denying their own citizens the "privileges and immunities" of American citizenship; as a result, in a series of cases interpreting the Amendment, the Supreme Court ruled that Americans are entitled to the same fundamental rights no matter which state they live in. You don't lose your right to choose your own religion or reading material, for example, when you move from one state to another. Today, when we refer to the Bill of Rights, we typically mean the first ten amendments plus the Equal Protection and Due Process clauses of the Fourteenth Amendment.

Because the Bill of Rights incorporates the Enlightenment understanding of liberty as a *negative*, that is, as our right to be free of government interference with our fundamental rights, *only the government* can violate the Constitution. If there has been no *state action*—the legal term meaning action taken by someone authorized to act on behalf of the government—the Constitution isn't involved.

Why It Matters

The Bill of Rights raises and answers an important procedural question: *who decides?* Who decides what prayer you say, what book you read, how many children you have? In our system, the government doesn't get to decide these and other very personal matters—we individuals decide these things for ourselves. The Bill of Rights doesn't tell us what we should value or how we should live our lives; it protects our right to make those decisions for ourselves, free of the interference of the government.

The Bill of Rights not only limits what the government can do, it limits what popular majorities can *vote* to have the government do. In fact, the Bill of Rights is sometimes called a "libertarian brake" on the power of the majority. The Bill of Rights ensures that a majority of your neighbors cannot vote to make you a Baptist or an Episcopalian; they also don't get to vote on your reading materials or your political opinions. When people don't understand that the Bill of Rights limits what majorities can vote to have the government do, they often misunderstand court decisions that uphold the right of individuals to hold unpopular positions or unconventional beliefs. The courts are not endorsing the choices made by those individuals; rather, they are protecting the right of individuals to make their own choices. When legislators fail to appreciate the limits imposed by the Bill of Rights, they often enact unconstitutional laws that deprive citizens of their liberties. When people don't understand the operation of the Fourteenth Amendment, they don't understand that the Bill of Rights applies to all levels of the government, including state and local authorities.

What Are Checks and Balances?

The US government is divided into three branches: executive (sometimes called administrative), legislative, and judicial. We refer to this constitutional structure, or architecture, as **separation of powers**, and it is fundamental to the American form of government.

The purpose of dividing government powers and responsibilities in this way was twofold. Enlightenment thinkers believed such a system would be more efficient, a division of labor that would make the best use of specialized skill and expertise. Judges would be better at judging if that was the bulk of their responsibilities; legislators would be more adept at passing laws, and so forth. They were also convinced that a division of power would keep any one branch from becoming too powerful and thus threaten the liberties of citizens. Each branch would *check* the powers of the other branches.

The legislative branch passes the laws. The executive branch administers those laws. And the judiciary branch—ultimately, the Supreme Court—determines whether the laws passed by legislators and the actions of the administration are consistent with the Constitution and Bill of Rights.

Checks and balances don't stop with the division of the federal government into three separate branches. The system devised by the Founders also gave significant authority to state and local units of the government, further dividing power. We call that structure *federalism*. If you have a zoning issue, for example, you take your case to your local municipal government; if you want to lobby for changes to family or marriage laws, you approach state legislators. Local, state, and federal authorities have different, although sometimes overlapping, jurisdictions. Federalism obviously raises the possibility of conflicts between federal and state laws; when that happens, the Constitution's **Supremacy Clause** provides that the federal law prevails. This division of authority between the federal government and the states has generated conflict ever since the issue caused the abandonment of the Articles of Confederation. We continue to struggle with the tension between those who believe that rules should be made by the government closest to the people and who thus promote states' rights and devolution of authority, and those whose concern for the need for consistency and uniformity among the states leads them to favor a stronger central government.

Why It Matters

Understanding the structure of our government is important for many reasons. If you want to effect a change, you need to know who has the authority to make that change. Griping about a zoning ordinance to a member of Congress may make you feel better, but it's not likely to do much good. Understanding how the branches interact is also necessary in order to cast informed votes; at election time, the airwaves are filled with political advertisements blaming officeholders for doing or failing to do something. Often, the effectiveness of that charge depends upon voters not understanding where the actual responsibility for action or inaction lies. This is particularly true of political campaigns for chief executives—governors or the president. People unfamiliar with checks and balances tend to believe that the president or governor can simply decide to make some change and it will happen. That is very rarely the case; even appointments to policymaking positions or the courts often require ratification by the legislative branch. We need to understand the operation of checks and balances and the way they limit the exercise of power in order to arrive at informed opinions about elected officials' performance.

What Is Judicial Independence?

In the federal courts, judges are appointed for life and can be removed only for improper behavior. This is an important part of our system of checks and balances. We elect a president who appoints members of the executive branch; we elect the men and women who represent us in Congress. Those two branches are thus "answerable" to voters. We can dismiss them—vote them out—if we don't like the way they discharge their duties. The courts, on the other hand, are not supposed to do voters' bidding; they are responsible to the Constitution and the rule of law, not to popular passions or the electorate.

Why It Matters

Removing judges from electoral politics insulates the courts from political pressure. When judges decide that previous interpretations of constitutional principles were wrong, or that new circumstances require modifying previous understandings of the law, people who were privileged under the previous interpretations often get agitated. When judges must decide high-profile or highly charged cases, we want them to make those decisions on the basis of their reading of the law, the facts, and the Constitution—not out of fear of being voted out of office by a public that may favor a different result. When judges are elected, as they are in some states, and must raise campaign money in order to mount a campaign, there is also a concern that they will weigh the positions of campaign contributors more heavily than the demands of justice or the requirements of the rule of law. When judges make poor decisions—and some will—we nevertheless want those decisions to be based upon their considered judgments, not on political expediency.

What Is Freedom of Speech?

Most of the people who want to ban a book or a painting, or who want to protect the flag **or the Virgin Mary from desecration**, are acting on their belief in the nature of the public good. They see unrestrained freedom as a threat to the social fabric. The Founders did not minimize the danger of bad ideas; they believed, however, that empowering the government to suppress "dangerous" or "offensive" ideas would be far more dangerous than the expression of those ideas—that once we hand over to the state the authority to decide which ideas have value, no ideas are safe. Where fundamental liberties are concerned, majority rule is a lot like poison gas—it's a great weapon until the wind shifts!

Like our legal and economic systems, the Free Speech Clause of the First Amendment is based upon a belief in the marketplace—if you make a better widget, it will beat out the competition; if you have a better idea, it will eventually emerge victorious. Accordingly, in our system, the antidote to bad speech is not suppression; it is more and better speech. Every so often, we must remind ourselves that the First Amendment was intended to protect *all* ideas, not just good ideas or those with which a majority or substantial minority may agree. As Justice Oliver Wendell Holmes memorably put it, the Free Speech Clause of the First Amendment was meant to **protect "the idea we hate."**

While the government must respect our right to express our own opinions—while it cannot control the content of our message—it *can* constitutionally regulate the time, place, and manner of that expression. Such restrictions, however—no sound trucks in residential neighborhoods after 10:00 p.m., for example—must be reasonable, must be content neutral (that is, not based upon the idea being expressed), and must apply to everyone equally.

There are also certain venues where the government has limited authority to regulate the content of speech. When the government is acting as an employer, for example, it can impose reasonable regulations on what employees can say while they are on the job. In public schools and public universities, the courts have ruled that administrators have an obligation to provide a sound educational environment, and have approved restrictions on expression deemed necessary to accomplish that.

Why It Matters

John Stuart Mill made perhaps the most enduring moral argument for free speech, writing, "If all mankind minus one were of one opinion, and only one person were of the contrary opinion, mankind would be no more justified in silencing that one person than he, if he had the power, would be justified in silencing mankind." This argument rests on respect for the integrity of the individual conscience—respect for the "inalienable" right of each individual to form and exchange opinions voluntarily, and to attempt to persuade others of the validity of those opinions. In addition to this argument for the importance of protecting free speech as an individual right, however, Mill and other Enlightenment philosophers believed that a robust "marketplace of ideas" was the mechanism most likely to guarantee that truth would emerge from public debate.

What Is Separation of Church and State?

The phrase **"separation of church and state" refers to the operation of the First Amendment's religion clauses.** The phrase itself does not appear in the Constitution. **Its first documented use was by Roger Williams, founder of Rhode Island, well before the Revolutionary War. The most famous use of the phrase came from Thomas Jefferson;** when Jefferson was president, a group of Danbury Baptists wrote to him asking for an official interpretation of the First Amendment's religion clauses. **Jefferson's response** was that the Establishment Clause and Free Exercise Clause were intended to "erect a wall of separation" between the government and religion.

Historians tell us that the Establishment Clause went through more than twenty drafts, with the Founders rejecting formulations such as "there shall be no National Church." The Establishment Clause prohibits the government from making any law "respecting an establishment of religion." The courts have uniformly held that this language not only forbids the government from establishing an official religion or state church but also prohibits government actions that *endorse or sponsor* religion, that favor one religion over another, or that prefer religion to nonreligion, or nonreligion over religion.

The Free Exercise Clause prohibits government interference with the "free exercise" of religion. Americans have the right to choose their own beliefs and to express those beliefs without fear of state disapproval.

Together, the Free Exercise Clause and the Establishment Clause require government *neutrality* in matters of religion. The government can neither *benefit* nor *burden* religious belief. One way to think about the operation of the religion clauses is that the Establishment Clause forbids the *public sector* (i.e., the government) from favoring or disfavoring religion, and the Free Exercise Clause forbids the government from interfering with the expression of religious beliefs in the *public square* (i.e., the myriad nongovernmental venues where citizens exchange ideas and opinions).

It's important to note that the courts have endorsed some restrictions on religious *observance* (as opposed to belief)—for example, your religion may call for sacrificing your firstborn, or for smoking dope, but your rights under the Free Exercise Clause don't extend that far!

Why It Matters

Some of Americans' most heated arguments are rooted in religion. This has always been the case, even in colonial times, when "religious diversity" mostly meant "different kinds of Protestant." As we become more religiously diverse as a nation, it becomes even more important to understand the constitutional limits on the rules that the government can impose.

When states misuse their authority to play favorites, to privilege some religious beliefs over others, people who do not share those privileged beliefs are relegated to the status of second-class citizens. Separation of church and state prevents adherents of majority religions from using the government to force their beliefs on others, and it keeps agencies of the government from interfering with the internal operations of churches, synagogues, and mosques. As the government becomes more pervasive, knowing where to draw the line between what is permissible and what is not becomes more difficult, making it even more important to understand the original purpose of the religion clauses.

As to that original purpose, there are few explanations better than the one offered by **John Leland**, an evangelical Baptist preacher with strong views on the individual's relationship to God, the inviolability of the individual conscience, and the limited nature of human knowledge. He wrote, **"Religion is a matter between God and individuals; religious opinions of men not being the objects of civil government, nor in any way under its control. . . . Government has no more to do with the religious opinions of men than it has with the principles of mathematics."**

What Is Freedom of the Press?

It is interesting to consider why freedom of the press was singled out for specific protection in the First Amendment. After all, the Free Speech Clause obviously protected journalists as well as other citizens. Why include a specific provision about freedom of the press?

The answer is that the architects of our Constitution believed that self-government requires the free and uninhibited flow of information. They wanted to be extra certain the government kept its hands off that information. So while the First Amendment protects all expression, the Free Press provision emphasizes the importance of protecting the specific kind of expression we call "journalism." Note that the Constitution doesn't protect persons called "journalists." It protects the *act* of journalism. The activity of "journalism" ensures the availability of information that is in the public interest.

The Founders were anything but naïve. They recognized that what they called the press and we call the media got it wrong a lot of the time. The newspapers of their own time were partisan rags that make our own politicized outlets look positively statesmanlike by comparison. But the Founders also believed that only the freest, most robust exchange of argument, information, and gossip would safeguard liberty. Neither freedom of speech nor freedom of the press rested on the notion that ideas are unimportant, that "sticks and stones can break my bones, but words won't hurt me." The Founders knew that ideas are often both powerful and dangerous. But they believed that giving the government power to determine which ideas and information can be transmitted or expressed was infinitely *more* dangerous.

Why It Matters

An informed citizenry is ultimately the only guarantor of liberty and sound public policy, and in our complex modern society, citizens depend upon the media for that information. This role of mass media is sometimes called "the watchdog function," and it is critically important to reasoned political decision making. One of the challenges facing American citizens in the age of the internet is the fragmenting of the traditional media and the loss of the fact-checking function it used to provide. When citizens do not have reliable and credible sources of information, ideology and partisanship drive the national conversation. Whatever their faults and shortcomings, the media providing what has been called "the journalism of verification" is critically important to democratic deliberation.

What Is the Right to Assemble?

In addition to the freedoms of speech, religion, and the press, the First Amendment provides for "the right of the people peaceably to assemble, and to petition the government for a redress of grievances." The right to assemble was firmly rooted in English law; it first appeared in the **Magna Carta**, which recognized the right of (certain) nobles to petition the king; much later, Parliament extended the right to every British subject. The US Supreme Court held in 1937 that the right to peaceably assemble "for lawful discussion, however unpopular the sponsorship, cannot be made a crime."

The right to assemble is not unlimited. The government has the right to impose content-neutral, reasonable time, place, and manner restrictions on demonstrations. The Supreme Court has held that government ownership of property does not automatically open that property to the public; in fact, the Court has given the government more authority to regulate expression when that expression takes place on government premises. For example, government officials can limit protests in public buildings such as courthouses and government offices in order to continue routine operations. When demonstrators plan to use public streets or sidewalks, local governments can require permits and designate routes in order to address traffic concerns and ensure public safety; however, permit restrictions and fees must be reasonable, and the government cannot refuse permits to disfavored groups, no matter how pernicious their message.

It's important to remember that the First Amendment protects the right to *peaceably* assemble. Protestors can be arrested for acts of civil disobedience, such as blocking traffic, or for other unlawful behaviors.

Why It Matters

When we think about assembling today, images of the Tea Party or Occupy Wall Street may come to mind, but this right to demonstrate, to engage in public protest, has been an important part of the American story for a long time. It protected union organizers and facilitated the civil rights movement of the late 1950s and early 1960s and the gay rights movement of our own times. It has also protected those who have tried to derail those movements. Demonstrations—sometimes called "symbolic speech"—are part of the broad umbrella of expressive freedom that the Founders believed to be essential to ordered liberty. Protecting the right of citizens to come together to protest perceived injustices or highlight social problems is yet another "check" on the power of the government. It empowers citizens to demand that their concerns be heard, if not necessarily addressed.

What Is Search and Seizure?

Before the American Revolution, British soldiers entered the homes of colonists at will, searching any person or place they wanted, often motivated by nothing more than political animosity. Resentment of this practice was a significant cause of the Revolution. To be fair, many Englishmen also objected to the use of "General Warrants" authorizing searches at the discretion of the authorities. William Pitt, addressing Parliament in 1763, famously said, "The poorest man may, in his cottage, bid defiance to all the forces of the Crown. It may be frail; its roof may shake; the wind may blow through it; the storm may enter; the rain may enter; but the King of England may not enter."

When America won independence, revulsion against such practices led to enactment of the Fourth Amendment, which provides that people have a right to be secure in their "persons, houses, papers and effects against unreasonable searches and seizures" and requires that police and other authorities have a warrant, issued upon "probable cause," to conduct such searches. The Amendment effectively prohibited searches unless the government had cause to believe that a crime had occurred and a good reason to believe that a specific person or place contained evidence of that crime. Furthermore, the reasonableness of the search was not to be left to the discretion of an individual policeman; a search warrant was to be issued by an *impartial* magistrate.

The courts have been faced with adapting the Fourth Amendment to the realities of modern American life, and many observers have voiced concern that those adaptations have weakened the Amendment's protections. Most Americans agree with the courts that it is impractical to require a police officer to obtain a warrant in cases where he has stopped a car and found probable cause to conduct a search. The courts' willingness to carve out exceptions to the Fourth Amendment in other circumstances, especially air travel and searches by the Transportation Safety Administration in the wake of 9/11, **continue to be debated.**

Why It Matters

The Fourth Amendment protects citizens against abuses of authority by erecting procedural safeguards against overreaching and intimidation. The United States, unlike totalitarian regimes, places the burden on the government to show why it should be allowed to search, rather than on citizens to demonstrate why they should be left alone. The Fourth Amendment rests on the premise that individuals are entitled to be left alone unless there is good reason, or **probable cause,** to intrude upon their privacy. It would thus violate the Fourth Amendment if police stationed themselves on a public street and demanded that every third passerby submit to a drug test, even if it could be demonstrated that a high percentage of those who lived in that neighborhood used drugs. The Fourth Amendment protects us against "fishing expeditions"—searches for something incriminating that are based solely on hunches, animosity, or cultural stereotypes.

What Is Due Process of Law?

The right of each citizen to "due process of law" is included in both the Fifth and Fourteenth Amendments. The Fifth Amendment provides that no person shall be "deprived of life, liberty, or property without due process of law," and the Fourteenth Amendment reinforces that prohibition by declaring that "no State shall make or enforce any law which shall abridge the privileges and immunities of citizens of the United States; nor shall any State deprive any person of life, liberty, or property without due process of law."

The effect of this insistence on a fair process can be seen most clearly in the American criminal justice system. **Unlike civil and canon law systems—sometimes referred to as *inquisitorial systems*—that were common in Europe at the time of the Revolutionary War, the American *adversarial system* requires** that proceedings be public rather than secretive, and gives the accused a presumption of innocence. In other words, the "burden of proof" is on the prosecution, which must prove guilt "beyond a reasonable doubt." The accused person need not prove his innocence. People charged with crimes have a right to be tried by a jury of their peers, in a trial presided over by an impartial judge, and they have the right to refuse to testify—to "take the Fifth," as popular culture phrases it. If the prosecution loses, that's it—the prohibition against double jeopardy means the state can't try again.

These and other aspects of criminal law's due process guarantees were efforts to address the imbalance between a powerful government and far less powerful individuals. The primary goal of our system is not to demonstrate the authority of an all-powerful state; it is to find the truth of a matter and achieve justice.

Americans' right to due process is not limited to the criminal justice system. Whenever the government acts in a way that threatens a citizen's liberty or property, the government must provide fair notice and an opportunity for that citizen to be heard. Due process in civil matters is based upon the individual's right to insist that government actions meet the test of *fundamental fairness*. So when the government proposes to take action that would violate what the courts have called "the liberty interest" (the right to enter into contracts, the right to engage in common occupations, the right to marry and bring up children, the right to worship freely, the right to acquire useful knowledge—in short, the right to enjoy the qualities of life recognized as essential to the pursuit of happiness), or when the government proposes to infringe a "property right" (licenses to practice a profession, social security entitlements, civil service employment), we have a right to be notified of the impending action and the reasons for it, as well as the right to argue about it—to confront witnesses against us and to have our arguments heard by an impartial decision maker.

There is one other type of due process, and it is widely misunderstood. This is **substantive due process**, sometimes called "the right to privacy." Substantive due process shields private rights from the exercise of arbitrary power; it distinguishes between matters that are properly a concern of the government, and thus subject to regulation, and those that are not. The Supreme Court has ruled, for example, that the question of whether married couples use birth control is a personal decision, not a decision that can constitutionally be made by the government.

Why It Matters

Due process is an essential element of the rule of law; the existence of a fair and open process that applies equally to everyone prevents the exercise of raw power and arbitrary or capricious enforcement of the rules. In addition to being seen as "fair play," due process is essential to social stability. When people feel that they have been treated unjustly, when they have been prevented from "having their say" or making their case, they are far less likely to abide by the law or official rulings.

Due process is also a tangible outgrowth of the Founders' insistence on limiting state power. The US Constitution draws a distinction between public and private, and substantive due process guarantees are one way we ensure that the government does not overreach, that it does not intrude into decisions that are properly left to individuals. Both procedural due process and substantive due process are meant to limit the authority of the government and prevent abuses of state power.

What Do We Mean by "Equal Protection of the Laws?"

Governments have to classify citizens for all kinds of perfectly acceptable reasons. We draw a distinction between children and adults, between motorists and pedestrians, between smokers and nonsmokers. The Equal Protection doctrine prevents the government from imposing *inappropriate* classifications—those based upon criteria that are irrelevant to the issue or that unfairly burden a particular group. The general rule is that a governmentally imposed classification must be *rationally related to a legitimate government interest*. A requirement that motorists observe a speed limit is clearly a classification related to the government's entirely proper interest in public safety. A law that imposed different speed limits on African American and Caucasian drivers would just as clearly be improper.

Laws can be discriminatory on their face (i.e., only white males can vote); however, these days, laws meant to be discriminatory are usually crafted to achieve that result *by design*. That is, they are drawn to look impartial on their face but to have a discriminatory effect. A rule that all firefighters weigh 180 or more pounds would prevent many more women from being employed than men, despite the fact that one's weight is not an indicator of strength or the ability to climb a ladder, and so on. There are also situations in which genuinely neutral laws are applied in a discriminatory fashion. The phrase "driving while black" grew out of statistics that suggest that some police officers were disproportionately stopping black motorists for speeding.

The courts will look more closely at classifications that burden constitutional rights, or that disadvantage members of groups that have historically been subject to discrimination. Racial minorities and women fall into those categories. We call that process of taking a closer look "heightened" or "strict" scrutiny.

Why It Matters

The constitutional requirement of equal protection is intended to prevent majorities from using the government to disadvantage individuals and minorities of whom the majority may disapprove. Equal Protection guarantees—like all the other provisions in the Bill of Rights—restrain only the government. Statutes may or may not address private-sector discrimination.

Essentially, the Equal Protection Clause requires the government to treat citizens as individuals, not as members of a group. Laws are supposed to be based upon a person's civic *behavior*, not gender, race, or other identity. So long as we citizens obey the laws, pay our taxes, and generally conduct ourselves in a way that does not endanger or disadvantage others, we are entitled to full equality with other citizens. That guarantee of equal civic rights is one of the aspects of American life that has been most admired around the globe; it has unleashed the productivity of previously marginalized groups and contributed significantly to American prosperity.

What Is the Difference between Civil Liberties and Civil Rights?

If you aren't quite certain about the difference between civil liberties and civil rights, you have a lot of company. The distinction is lost on many, if not most, citizens, as well as a good number of legislators. *Civil liberties* are the individual freedoms protected by the Bill of Rights. They are rights that agencies of government must respect. Citizens of the new United States refused to ratify the Constitution unless a Bill of Rights was added that would specifically protect citizens against *official* infringements of their rights. Among our civil liberties are the right to free expression, the right to worship—or not—as we choose, and the right to be free from unreasonable searches and seizures. After the Civil War, the Fourteenth Amendment added the Equal Protection Clause, which prohibits the government from treating equally situated citizens unequally. Only the government can violate your civil liberties.

Civil rights took a lot longer to achieve and were—and still are—a lot more controversial. Congress passed the **Civil Rights Act** in 1964. Civil rights laws protect people against *private* acts of discrimination in employment, housing, and education. The original Civil Rights Act applied to businesses engaged in interstate commerce—businesses that held themselves out to be "public accommodations" but were, shall we say, "selective" about which segments of the public they were willing to accommodate. State and local civil rights acts followed passage of the federal law. Civil rights laws generally include a list of characteristics that cannot be used to disfavor or discriminate against people: race, religion, gender, and so forth.

Why It Matters

Knowing the difference between rights that are rooted in the Constitution and those that are creations of statute helps Americans better understand our national history and the arguments being made by groups that remain unprotected by civil rights laws. For example, gay, lesbian, bisexual, and transgender people in states with civil rights laws that do not prohibit discrimination on the basis of sexual orientation can legally be fired just for being gay. Landlords can refuse to rent apartments to them. The Fourteenth Amendment's Equal Protection Clause prohibits government employers from treating gays and lesbians differently, but it has nothing to say about private employers.

Similarly, knowing which rights are constitutionally protected should allay concerns expressed by some religious groups that passage of a civil rights law will force them to change their religious practices. Since the Free Exercise Clause is a *constitutional* guarantee, the amendment of a civil rights measure to include protection for gays and lesbians would have no effect on the practices or preaching of churches that consider homosexuality sinful—just as civil recognition of divorce did not mean that the Catholic Church had to change its theological opposition to that practice.

CHAPTER 2

What Everyone Should Know about the American Economic System

What Is Capitalism?

CAPITALISM IS DEFINED as an economic and political system in which a country's trade and industry are controlled by private owners for profit. It is characterized by free markets, where the prices of goods and services are determined by supply and demand rather than set by the government. Economists often define the ideal of free trade as a transaction between a willing buyer and a willing seller, both of whom are in possession of all the information relevant to that transaction.

Why It Matters

Understanding the importance of free trade to capitalism is important because it defines the proper role of government in a capitalist system—as an "umpire" or "referee," ensuring that everyone plays by the rules. (Those rules or regulations are a distinct form of state action.) For example, Teddy Roosevelt reminded us that monopolies distort markets; if one company can dominate a market, that company can dictate prices and other terms, with the result that those transactions will no longer be truly voluntary. If Manufacturer A can avoid the cost of disposing the waste produced by his factory by dumping it into the nearest river, he will be able to compete unfairly with Manufacturer B, who is following the rules governing proper waste disposal. If Chicken Farmer A is able to control his costs and gain market share by failing to keep his coops clean and his chickens free of disease, unwary consumers will become ill. Most economists agree that in order for markets to operate properly, the government must act as an umpire, ensuring a level playing field.

This need for the government is a response to what economists call **"market failure."** There are three situations in which **Adam Smith's "invisible hand"** doesn't work: when monopolies or corrupt practices replace competition; when so-called externalities such as pollution harm people who aren't party to the transaction (who are neither buyer nor seller); and when there are "information asymmetries"—that is, when buyers don't have access to information they need to bargain in their own interest. Since markets don't have built-in mechanisms for dealing with these situations, most economists argue that regulation is needed.

Economists and others often disagree about the need for particular regulations, but most do agree that an absence of all regulatory activity undermines capitalism. Unregulated markets can lead to a different system, sometimes called *corporatism*. In corporatist systems, government regulations favoring powerful corporate interests are the result of lobbying by corporate and moneyed special interests that stand to benefit from them. You might think of it as a football game where one side has paid the referee to make calls favorable to that team.

What Is Socialism?

Socialism is the collective provision of goods and services. The decision of whether to pay for certain services collectively rather than to leave their production and consumption to the free market can be based upon a number of factors. First, there are some goods that free markets cannot or will not produce. Economists call them *public goods* and define them as both "non-excludable," meaning that individuals who haven't paid for them cannot be effectively kept from using them, and "nonrivalrous," meaning that use by one person does not reduce the availability of that good to others. Examples of public goods include fresh air, knowledge, lighthouses, national defense, flood control systems, and street lighting. If we are to have these goods, they must be supplied by the whole society, usually through the government, and paid for with tax dollars.

Not all goods and services that we provide collectively are public goods. Policymakers have often based decisions to socialize services on other considerations: we socialize police and fire protection because doing so is generally more efficient and cost-effective, and because most of us believe that limiting such services only to people who can afford to pay for them would be immoral. We socialize garbage collection in more densely populated urban areas in order to enhance the livability of our cities and to prevent disease transmission.

Why It Matters

Getting the "mix" right between goods that we provide collectively and those that we leave to the free market is important because too much socialism hampers economic health. Just as unrestrained capitalism can become corporatism, socializing the provision of goods that the market can supply reduces innovation and incentives to produce. During the twentieth century, many countries experimented with efforts to socialize major areas of their economies, and even to implement socialism's extreme—communism—with uniformly poor results. Not only did economic productivity suffer, so did political freedom. When governments have too much control over the means of production and distribution, they can easily become authoritarian.

Virtually all countries today have mixed economies, with elements of both private and state enterprise. The challenge is getting the right balance between socialized and free market provision of goods and services.

What Are the Differences among Socialism, Fascism, and Communism?

In our highly polarized politics today, words like "socialism," "fascism," and "communism" are used more as insults than descriptions. There are also numerous disagreements about the essential characteristics of these systems, probably because the theories underlying them are so different from the actual experiences of those who tried them.

Socialism may be the least precise of these terms. It is generally applied to mixed economies where the social safety net is much broader and the tax burden is correspondingly higher than in the United States—Scandinavian countries are an example.

Communism begins with the belief that equality is defined by equal results; this is summed up in the **well-known adage, "From each according to his ability; to each according to his needs."** All property is owned communally, by everyone (hence the term "communism"). In practice, this meant that all property was owned by the government, ostensibly on behalf of the people. In theory, communism erases all class distinctions, and wealth is redistributed so that everyone gets the same share. In practice, the government controls the means of production, and most individual decisions are made by the state. Since the quality and quantity of work is divorced from reward, there is less incentive to innovate or produce, and, ultimately, countries that have tried to create a communist system have collapsed (the USSR) or moved toward a more mixed economy (China).

Fascism is sometimes called "national socialism," but it differs significantly from socialism. The most striking aspect of fascist systems is the elevation of the nation—a fervent nationalism is central to fascist philosophy. There is a union between business and the state; although there is nominally private property, the government controls business decisions. Fascist regimes tend to be focused on a (glorious) past, and to uphold traditional class structures and gender roles that are believed necessary to maintain the social order.

Three elements commonly identified with fascism are (1) a national identity fused with racial/ethnic identity and concepts of racial superiority; (2) rejection of civil liberties and democracy in favor of authoritarian government; and (3) aggressive militarism. Fascism has been defined by this radical authoritarian nationalism, with fascists seeking to unify the nation through the elevation of the state over the individual, and the mass mobilization of the national community through discipline, indoctrination, and physical training. Nazi Germany and Mussolini's Italy are the most notable examples of fascist regimes.

Why It Matters

Understanding the differences among these different political philosophies is important for two reasons: First, we cannot have productive discussions or draw appropriate historical analogies if we don't have common understandings of the words we are using. Second, we cannot learn from history and the mistakes of the past if the terms we are using are unconnected to any substantive content. When activists accuse an American president of being a fascist or a communist—labels that have been thrown at both President George W. Bush and President Barack Obama—it trivializes the **crimes committed by the Nazis** and the Soviets and makes it difficult, if not impossible, to engage in reasoned discussion about—or persuasive criticism of—whatever the president is doing that led to the charge.

What Are the Differences among the Private, Nonprofit, and Public Sectors?

Again, this may seem like a silly question—much like "what is government?"—but in an era of blurring boundaries, it is important to recognize the distinctions between the sectors. The public sector is composed of the government at all levels—local, state, and federal. If it is the government, it is part of the public sector (not to be confused with the public *square*, which is not a sector at all, but a shorthand phrase meaning the arenas where public debates occur). Both the nonprofit and private sectors are private in the sense that they are not the government, but the nonprofit sector—sometimes referred to as "civil society"—is composed of voluntary associations dedicated to providing a public good that the organization itself has chosen to pursue rather than generating a profit. Nonprofit organizations are sometimes said to provide a buffer between impersonal government agencies, on the one hand, and individuals and their families, on the other. They range from professional associations to charitable organizations to religious communities and volunteer groups. Technically, the private sector is everything other than government and nonprofit and voluntary associations, but usually the term is employed to mean for-profit business enterprises.

Why It Matters

Knowing whether a particular enterprise is part of the government, a nonprofit organization, or a private, for-profit entity tells us a great deal about its mission and purpose, because the sectors have very different operating assumptions and philosophies. The government, as we have seen, is the collective mechanism through which communities and nations provide services either that cannot be provided privately or that policymakers have determined should be provided by the state. Nonprofit organizations also have a social mission, either supplementing government services deemed to be inadequate or providing something that the government is not providing or cannot provide. Private sector enterprises exist to earn a profit. While we want the government and charitable organizations to operate in a businesslike manner, those sectors are not businesses. They are fundamentally different from for-profit entities and pose very different management challenges.

One of the major debates among policymakers involves the effect of outsourcing (sometimes called privatization) on sector identity. Some scholars worry that too much government outsourcing—especially to non-profit organizations—is both "hollowing out" the government's capacity to manage core government responsibilities and turning nonprofits into less visible arms of the state. Knowing the differences between sectors and their missions allows citizens to monitor such practices.

What Are Taxes and How Are They Assessed?

Taxes have been called the price we pay for membership in society. How we tax, who we tax, and how much we tax are probably the most hotly debated political issues we confront, because what seems fair to one person seems unfair to another. Most people agree that governments need revenue in order to provide services, but they don't necessarily agree on the services that the government should provide, the amount of revenue the government really needs, or the way the government should go about raising that money.

Federal, state, and local governments all have the power to tax, and policymakers must decide *what* to tax (earned income, dividends and interest, property, sales, inheritances?), *who* to tax (nonprofits, for-profits, individuals, corporations?), and *how* to tax (progressively, regressively, proportionately?). Governments also must decide how much will be spent and for what, in order to determine how much money must be raised through the tax system. All of these decisions, and their economic consequences are the subject of heated and legitimate debate.

Why It Matters

Americans believe passionately in fairness and equality. The tax system may be complicated, and taxing and spending decisions may be difficult to understand, but a basic knowledge of what the money goes for, how much goes where, and where it comes from is essential if we are to have productive discussions about tax fairness. For example, surveys routinely show that large percentages of Americans believe we spend 25 percent of the federal budget on foreign aid, and that a "more appropriate" amount would be 10 percent. **However, we actually spend slightly more than *1 percent* on foreign aid.**

The American tax system depends upon the voluntary compliance of taxpayers. No constable comes to your door to check your books and calculate what you owe, although you may be audited if your tax return raises red flags. If the system is to work, if we expect people to report their incomes accurately and pay what they owe without coercion, the system must be viewed as fundamentally fair. Widespread misconceptions erode the public's belief in the system's legitimacy and encourage tax evasion.

One of the most important misunderstandings of our tax system concerns the difference between the *marginal tax rate* and the *effective tax rate*. In a progressive tax system, reported income is divided into brackets. The marginal rate is the rate applied to dollars earned that fall in successively higher brackets. For example, let's assume you earn $60,000, and there are no exemptions or other adjustments—that the whole $60,000 is being taxed. If the first $20,000 of income you earn falls in a 10 percent bracket, that first $20,000 will always be taxed at 10 percent, or $2,000, no matter how much more you earn. If the next $20,000 is taxed at the next highest rate—say 15 percent—you will pay $3,000 on that $20,000, and if the *next* $20,000 is taxed at 20 percent, that amount will be taxed $4,000. Using this (grossly oversimplified) example, your *marginal* rate is 20 percent, but your *effective* rate—the actual percentage of your total earnings that you pay in taxes—is 15 percent. Your total tax, using this example, would be $9,000; if you were paying 20 percent on the entire $60,000, your tax bill would be $12,000. In real life, thanks to multiple exemptions, deductions, and tax incentives, people who make income subject to the highest current marginal tax bracket—36 percent—can bring their effective rates down dramatically. Millionaires often have an effective tax rate below 15 percent.

Many people understand this but many others do not. When they read about the marginal rates of 50 percent or even 90 percent that used to be in effect, they think those rates were applied to the taxpayer's entire earnings.

Another widespread misconception concerns the identification of federal taxes with the income taxes. Personal income taxes are federal taxes, but there are **many other kinds of federal tax**: payroll tax, federal excise tax, and various specialized taxes. While the income tax is mildly *progressive*—that is, as income rises into successive tax brackets, it is subject to higher rates—taxes like the payroll tax and federal excise tax on gasoline are considered *regressive* because they take a larger percentage of the income of those who earn less. Furthermore, people who earn very little money and people with lots of deductions may not pay income tax, but almost everyone pays payroll and excise taxes.

What Is the Difference between the Deficit and the Debt?

The deficit is the difference between the revenues the government takes in (receipts) and what it spends (outlays) on an annual basis. Receipts are all of the money the federal government takes in from income, excise and social insurance taxes, fees, and other income. Outlays are all federal spending, including social security and Medicare benefits, defense spending, administering the federal government and all its programs, and interest payments on the debt. When annual outlays exceed revenues, there is a deficit, and the Treasury must borrow the money needed for the government to pay its bills. It does so by selling securities and savings bonds to the general public and other willing buyers both in the United States and abroad. Additionally, the government trust funds are required by law to invest accumulated surpluses in Treasury securities. Securities issued to the public and to the government trust funds then become part of the total debt. The national debt is composed of accumulated deficits.

Why It Matters

Although pundits like to compare federal spending to the way individuals manage our households, the comparison is not really very apt or very helpful, because money that the government spends has a large effect on the economy and job creation. Most economists—conservative or liberal— advise the government to spend more and tax less during economic downturns in order to lift economic performance. (Both government spending and tax cuts will stimulate the economy, although economists debate which approach is more likely to stimulate demand.) On the other hand, too much debt accumulated over too long a period can depress economic productivity by driving up the cost of business and personal borrowing, among other things. When government programs are cut too deeply in order to save money, jobs in the private and nonprofit sectors are lost with a corresponding loss of tax revenues. This is one concern with our defense budget, for example. Even though the Pentagon has determined we don't need to spend so much, large-scale contractors with thousands of employees depend upon defense contracts for their existence. In order to accurately assess proposals being made by our elected officials, it is important to understand whether we are talking about long-term or short-term spending, and to understand what the effects of suggested reductions or increases in spending are likely to be.

What Is the Debt Ceiling?

The Constitution requires that Congress make all spending decisions—the president proposes but Congress disposes. Sometimes, as we've seen, Congress authorizes more spending than the government collects in revenue. That requires the government to borrow the difference in order to cover the deficit that Congress has authorized. For reasons that are not entirely clear, Congress also votes to authorize borrowing that will exceed the previously set debt limit, or ceiling. This may seem a bit silly, since that vote comes from the same Congress that has already voted for the spending that requires the borrowing, but this practice of raising the debt ceiling has generally been uncontroversial, and for years the ceiling has been raised by votes from large bipartisan majorities. More recently, a significant minority of representatives has refused to vote to raise the ceiling.

Why It Matters

It is unclear why some in the House of Representatives refuse to cast the previously pro forma vote to raise the debt ceiling, since failing to raise the debt ceiling would not do anything to reduce the national debt. Instead, it would be a vote for the United States to default on what it owes. If Congress were actually to fail to raise the ceiling, the results would be catastrophic; such an act would require the United States to stop paying many of its bills—including amounts owed to senior citizens for social security, defense contractors and members of the military who defend the country, and many others. Economists warn that such a failure to pay our bills could precipitate a worldwide economic collapse.

CHAPTER 3

What Everyone Should Know about Science

What Is Science?

SCIENCE HAS BEEN DEFINED as the pursuit of knowledge and understanding of the natural and social world following a systematic methodology based on evidence. It requires the observation, identification, description, experimental investigation, and theoretical explanation of natural phenomena. Science is generally characterized by *empirical inquiry*; understood in this way, modern science dates back to the Enlightenment, when figures like Isaac Newton and Robert Boyle applied *inductive reasoning* to the methodological study of the physical world. The scientific method begins with the identification of a question or problem, after which relevant data are gathered, a **hypothesis** is formulated based upon that data, and the hypothesis is then subject to additional empirical testing.

Why It Matters

Understanding what human activities can be classified as scientific, rather than philosophical, ideological, or religious, is the only way we can determine the appropriate jurisdiction of governmental activities. If the House of Representatives' Committee on Science and Technology is to properly evaluate matters that come before it, members of the committee need to understand what counts as science and what does not. When public school boards are asked to include alternate theories of planetary and human creation in science curricula, they need to be able to distinguish between theories that are scientific—and thus appropriate for inclusion in a science classroom—and those that are based upon religious doctrine rather than empirical investigation.

What Is a Scientific Theory?

Development of a scientific theory is a part of the scientific method. It involves summarizing a group of hypotheses that have been successfully and repeatedly tested. Once enough evidence accumulates to support a hypothesis, a theory is developed, and that theory becomes accepted as a valid explanation of a particular phenomenon. Scientific theories must be based on careful examination of the facts.

In the scientific method, a clear distinction is drawn between facts, which can be observed and/or measured, and theories, which are scientists' explanations and interpretations of the facts. Scientists can draw various interpretations from their observations, or from the results of their experiments, but the facts, which have been called the cornerstone of the scientific method, do not change. A theory must include statements that have what scientists call "observational consequences." A good theory, like Newton's theory of gravity, will also have *unity*, which means it consists of a limited number of problem-solving strategies that can be applied to a wide range of scientific circumstances. A sound theory consists of a number of hypotheses that can be tested independently. A scientific theory is not the end result of the scientific method; theories are constantly supported or rejected, improved or modified as more information is gathered so that the accuracy of the prediction becomes greater over time. In order to be considered scientific, hypotheses and theories are always subject to *falsification*.

Why It Matters

In everyday conversation, the word "theory" means something very different from its scientific meaning. Nonscientists use the word "theory" to mean "speculation" or "guess"—"I have a theory about that." When we fail to distinguish between our casual use of the term and its very different scientific meaning, we confuse discussions of science policy and science education. This has been particularly true of arguments surrounding Darwin's theory of evolution. Some religious people believe that the theory of evolution is inconsistent with a belief in God (although other religious authorities disagree). They challenge the teaching of evolution in biology classes because they believe that it is "just a theory." Such debates are seldom enlightening because participants are using the same term to mean very different things; they are talking past each other.

What Is Falsification?

Falsification is an essential characteristic of a scientific hypothesis or theory. Basically, a falsifiable assertion is one that can be empirically refuted or disproved. Falsifiability means that the hypothesis is testable by empirical experiment, and that it thus conforms to the standards of the scientific method. Merely because something is "falsifiable" does not mean it is false; rather, it means that *if* it is false, then observation or experiment will at some point demonstrate its falsity.

Why It Matters

It is important to understand that many things may be true, or generally accepted as true, without being falsifiable. Observing that a woman or a sunset is beautiful, asserting that you feel sad, declaring that you are in love, and similar statements may be very true, but they aren't science—because they can't be falsified—they cannot be empirically proved or disproved. Similarly, God may exist, but that existence is not falsifiable—God cannot be dragged into a laboratory and tested. One either believes in his existence or not. That's why religious belief is called *faith*.

CHAPTER 4

What Everyone Should Know about Politics

What Is Partisanship?

WHEN THE US CONSTITUTION was drafted and ratified, there were no political parties. James Madison, for one, was highly skeptical of parties and "**factions**." Nevertheless, he and Thomas Jefferson would go on to found the Democratic-Republican Party in opposition to the Federalist Party. *Partisanship*—understood as actions taken to advance the fortunes of one's own party at the expense of the opposing one—has been a feature of the American political landscape ever since. Over the years, the degree of polarization has ebbed and flowed, and the parties themselves have often changed their character and even their names.

From time to time, factions unhappy with the direction of both their own party and the opposition have broken off to form a third party—we've seen the Prohibition Party, the Progressive Party, the Bull-Moose Party, the American Independent Party, and more recently, the Green Party and the Libertarians, among others. These parties rarely gain much traction; they face too many systemic obstacles. For example, state laws typically provide that Democratic and Republican candidates automatically get on the ballot, whereas third-party candidates usually have to get thousands of signatures on petitions in order to do so. (Democratic and Republican officials have an obvious incentive to protect the two-party system.)

Why It Matters

Historically, the two major parties have tended to be "big tents," each encompassing a fairly wide array of political ideologies and opinions. From time to time, however, the parties polarize—literally, "go toward their poles"—and take deeply opposing approaches to governing and the hot-button issues of the day. When that happens, moderate and middle-of-the-road Americans often feel ill at ease in either party; they feel that they have been effectively disenfranchised. America's worst episode of political polarization was the schism over slavery that led to the Civil War, but the battle lines drawn between today's Republicans and Democrats are deep enough to justify substantial concern because the current level of polarization is causing significant dysfunction at both the state and federal level.

In order for any level of government to operate efficiently, elected officials must agree on basic principles, goals, and priorities; when such agreement is lacking, we get government shutdowns, political "dirty tricks" (as one party or the other tries to gain advantage by fair means or foul), and wasted opportunities to address the issues that most Americans care about. Recent political polarization has been worsened by the activities of so-called Super PACs (associations of moneyed interests that were created in response to the Supreme Court's decision in **Citizens United v. Federal Election Commission**, which allowed corporations and unions to make virtually unlimited political donations) and by the internet and social media, which have facilitated political organizing and fund-raising but have also vastly increased the prevalence of political "spin" and misinformation.

What Are the Obligations of Citizenship?

If you belong to a club, you understand that you need to pay your dues. Citizenship is no different. Everyone who lives in the United States accepts the benefits that local, state, and federal government provides. Taxes are one part of the "dues" we pay for those benefits, but citizens also have an obligation to participate in the democratic process and to base that participation on sound information. That means fact-checking the letter your uncle forwarded from the internet confirming his latest political theory, listening carefully to the political arguments of candidates for public office, and voting for the people you believe are best suited to make decisions that will affect us all.

Why It Matters

Basing our political decisions and votes on accurate information doesn't necessarily mean Americans will agree about politics or policies. But more informed discussions are also more likely to be productive—and civil—discussions. America could certainly use a change of tone right now.

* * *

Patriotism and unity of national purpose do not require uniformity of opinion; humans will inevitably bring different motives and perspectives to our common endeavors, and people of good will can quite often differ. What is important is not that Americans all agree; what is important is *how* we disagree. Our disputes need to be grounded in fact and conducted in ways that are intellectually honest, fair-minded, and open to consideration of different interpretations and perspectives. The old (overused but pertinent) adage is right: It isn't whether you win or lose, it's how you play the game. In the long run, all of us will benefit from discussions conducted with more light and less heat.

If this publication helps even a few people conduct more reasoned and civil disputes, it will serve its purpose.

About the Author

SHEILA SUESS KENNEDY is professor of law and public policy at the School of Public and Environmental Affairs at Indiana University–Purdue University Indianapolis (IUPUI). She is a Faculty Fellow with both the Center for Religion and American Culture and the Tobias Center for Leadership Excellence, and an adjunct professor of political science. She holds a JD with honors from Indiana University, where she was managing editor of the *Indiana Law Review*. Kennedy's research interests focus on constitutional culture, civil liberties / civil rights, and religion and public policy, and she has authored many books and articles on these subjects. Before joining the university in 1998, Kennedy practiced real estate, administrative, and business law in Indianapolis, first with Baker & Daniels and later as a partner with Mears, Crawford, Kennedy & Eichholz. She was corporation counsel for the City of Indianapolis from 1977 to 1979, was the Republican candidate for Indiana's then 11th congressional district seat in 1980, and subsequently served as president of Kennedy Development Services. Prior to joining the faculty at IUPUI, she spent six years as executive director of the Indiana Affiliate of the American Civil Liberties Union. Kennedy has won numerous awards, most recently Outstanding Faculty in Public Service, awarded by the Indiana Association for Public Service, and the IUPUI Chancellor's Faculty Award for Excellence in Civic Engagement.

CPSIA information can be obtained at www.ICGtesting.com
Printed in the USA
LVOW11s1551201016

509596LV00005B/844/P